Working o

A Practical Guide to Mental Health

Karl Shallowhorn

To Robin –
Thanks for being
with me on my
journey. Be well!
Peace

chipmunkapublishing

the mental health publisher

Published by

Chipmunkapublishing

PO Box 6872

Brentwood

Essex CM13 1ZT

United Kingdom

http://www.chipmunkapublishing.com

Chipmunkapublishing gratefully acknowledge the support of Arts Council England.

Acknowledgments

I would like to thank several people without whom this manual would not be possible. First, I thank my parents and extended family for their unwavering support during the times when all they had was their hope and prayers for a better life for me. I thank my wife Suzy for being by my side as the best friend I could ever hope for, and my daughters Sarah and Lillie for teaching me how to think of others and not be so selfish. I'd also like to acknowledge a debt of gratitude to all of the therapists with whom I've had the opportunity to work with for nearly 30 years and especially to Jane, who has always been a source of trust and sound judgment.

For their editorial assistance, I'd like to thank The Rev. Susan A. Blain, Lawrence Van Heusen, Tom McNulty, and Lucia Miller of the Mental Illness Education Project.

Finally, I'd be remiss if I did not express my gratitude to the God of my understanding for never abandoning me even in my darkest days.

Karl Shallowhorn

Author Biography

Karl Shallowhorn was born in Buffalo, NY in 1962. He was diagnosed with Bipolar Disorder in 1981 and spent nearly 15 years struggling with his disease before stabilizing his condition. Karl is a recovering addict and a New York State Credentialed Alcoholism and Substance Abuse Counselor currently working at Horizon Health Services. He has a Master of Science Degree in Student Personnel Administration from Buffalo State College.

Karl's experience as both a consumer and clinician have given him a keen perspective on what is needed to both manage symptoms and go beyond one's self-perceived limitations. Karl has done numerous presentations on mental health for the WNY Children's Psychiatric Center, Action for Mental Health, Mental Health Peer Connection, and the Buffalo Chapter of the National Alliance on Mental Illness. He is also on the team of Campus Outreach Services, a U.S.-based speakers' bureau. In November 2010 he appeared on the WJYE-FM radio program, "Spotlight on Health" and in 2008 he was a recipient of the Erie County Disabilities Employment Recognition Award. He is married with two daughters and lives with his family in Amherst, NY.

Karl Shallowhorn

Introduction

I have been living with bipolar disorder (BP) since 1981 and while the early part of my journey was tumultuous, I have been able to find a way to face my illness head-on and lead a stable life. I have been hospitalized at several Buffalo mental health facilities. I have been prescribed a variety of psychiatric medications over the years including Lithium and Thioridazine (Mellaril), which I've been taking for much of my life.

When I was initially diagnosed with BP I was complicating my condition by abusing drugs and alcohol. This certainly did not help. I was very confused and lacked any concrete guidance on how to address my disease. I was in counseling; however I was non-compliant with treatment methods and any efforts to help me went by the wayside.

During this period in the 80's, when I was lost in the disease, I still had hoped that I could someday have a life that resembled some sense of normalcy. I would often fantasize about having a "real" job and family of my own. I just wanted the pain to stop.

I was extremely fortunate to have parents that loved me no matter what. I am an only child and was adopted at an early age. This permitted my parents to focus much of their time and energy into helping me recover. My folks were there for me every step of the way. My mom, however, did eventually stop visiting me in the hospital. It was too much for her to bear seeing me under those conditions. Fortunately she lived long enough to see me get back on my feet.

During my early recovery I experienced a wide variety of treatment modalities: psychotherapy with psychiatrists, licensed clinicians, outpatient group therapy, day treatment, and, inpatient treatment. I believe that they all have their individual merits. I decided to write this manual so I could share with others what has worked for me. I realize that recovery can be case-specific however I do believe that there are many common denominators in successful mental health treatment. I hope to reflect on some of these methods coupled with my past and present experience to demonstrate how recovery is possible.

What I want to communicate in this manual is that *recovery is possible*. One of the key elements is learning when to ask for help. I had to learn this the hard way. By asking for help from others we are able to acknowledge that we don't have all of the answers. When we open ourselves to the help of others we are able to find the way to realize the life that we would like to live.

The Journey

My journey of living with bipolar disorder began in 1980. I was a student at college in Central Michigan. Shortly after beginning classes I started to experiment with marijuana. I already had a history of alcohol abuse from high school. In the January term, my academic performance suffered greatly due to my drug and alcohol use. At that time I became symptomatic – paranoia and confusion were regular occurrences. I recognize here the start of a continuing pattern, substance abuse complicating my BP symptoms.

It all came to a head in the winter of 1981. My life was crumbling around me. On Friday, February 13, I cut my wrists and descended into a major psychotic episode. I was delusional, thinking that I was the devil. I became catatonic and was discovered in my dorm room by the residence director and a school security guard. I was taken to the Flint Hurley Medical Center and was admitted to the psych unit. My parents were notified and they came to retrieve me. I was taken back to Buffalo and immediately admitted to the Buffalo General Hospital (BGH) psychiatric unit for those most severely affected with mental illness. I was a mere shell of the person I used to be. Confused and afraid, I didn't have any sense of reality; I didn't even know who I was.

It was a tremendously difficult recovery. Slowly, I began to regain some sense of who I was. Honestly, I do not even know how long I was there. I was discharged and began to see a private psychiatrist who attempted to quell my symptoms with medication. Eventually I felt well enough to try to return to school the next fall. Just before the fall semester began I met a guy who offered to get me high, which I did, unaware of the connection between my drug use and mental health problems. I guess you could say that I was in denial. This initiated another manic episode within about 3 months and another visit to BGH.

This was the cycle my life took for several years to come. I was admitted to the Buffalo Psychiatric Center (BPC) on three occasions in the early 80's and during one of these times I was given ECT – electroconvulsive therapy. Most of my episodes were of the manic variety with delusional features. The "Psych Center", as it was affectionately called, was a pretty scary place to be. During my time there I was in a unit for men with severe persistent mental illness. From what I recall, some of these men were considered to be criminally insane and unable to transition to life on the outside. I hated it there.

I had one major depressive episode in the summer of 1983 when I spent most of that season in bed and incapable of functioning. This preceded my last visit to BPC. The following January I enrolled at Buffalo State College. Ironically, Buffalo State is located right next door to BPC. During my time as a student there I was consistently reminded of my history at BPC. This did not, however, deter me from drug use, which served as a catalyst for my mental and emotional relapse.

Miraculously, I managed to graduate from Buffalo State in 1987 with a degree in Broadcasting. During my time at BSC I had aspired to work in radio.

I had spent several years working at WBNY, the college radio station. Music has always been a comfort to me. It has always been there to affect my mood, usually in a good way. Upon graduation, I was able to land a job at a Buffalo-based recording studio that specialized in producing local bands as well as radio commercials. My mental illness was in remission during this period although I was still dabbling in drugs and alcohol.

I had been going to Horizon Health Services, a Western New York treatment agency, for over five years with limited success in managing my bipolar disorder. In 1985 I was assigned to a counselor named Dick whom I really connected with. Dick was a Vietnam vet who was able to break through my defenses of denial and ambivalence. He repeatedly advised me to attend 12 Step meetings. Finally, on January 13, 1988 I had a session with Dick. During the session he essentially told me that I had three choices: go to rehab, go to a 12-Step meeting or end up back in the hospital. I decided to surrender and go to the 12-Step meeting.

I vividly recall the experience. Earlier in the day a friend called me to see if I would be willing to drive him to a dealer's house to buy some weed. I agreed and was given a joint as payment for the deed that had been done. My folks had gone out for the evening so I decided to smoke half the joint saving the rest for later. Under the influence, I drove out to the meeting. It was a frigid night and I was pretty nervous not knowing what to expect. I pulled into the church parking lot and saw a number of cars. I parked, turned off the car and proceeded to make my way to the church hall where the meeting was being held. I walked up to the door and looked through the glass. Inside, I saw a number of young people – all talking, some smiling and laughing. At this moment I was convinced that this must be some kind of church youth group. "Where are all the junkies?" I asked myself.

Convinced that I was in the wrong place, I turned and went back to my car. I got inside and sat frozen with my hands on the steering wheel. "What should I do?" I asked myself. I couldn't just go to my next session with Dick and tell him that I didn't make the meeting. Then, a car pulled up nearby. I decided to see what was really happening. I walked over to the young man getting out of his car and asked, "Hey, do you know what's going on inside?"

"Yeah," he replied, "it's a [12-Step] meeting."

"Oh, okay," I responded and we walked into the meeting together.

This experience opened my eyes to a world that I honestly never knew existed - a world without drugs. At that first meeting I began to feel an overwhelming sense of hope. That night I recall seeing addicts standing up a celebrating various lengths of clean time. The simple fact that someone could string even 30 days together was beyond me. This was what I had been looking for – an opportunity to turn my life around.

Unfortunately I was still experiencing manic tendencies during my first year clean from alcohol and drugs. I was having racing thoughts and delusions. In April 1989 I was admitted to the hospital once again, this time at the Erie County Medical

Center. This was difficult to bear. I had thought that since I had stopped getting high that my mental illness would be arrested, but I was wrong. This time, however, I did have the support of not only my family but also my new-found friends in recovery. During that period I remember calling my sponsor Dave at all times of the night and he patiently would talk me down until I was able to sleep.

During that next year or so I worked a series of temp jobs, filling time while I got my head together. Finally, in 1990, I decided to return to school to pursue a career in Alcoholism Counseling. I attended Erie Community College and in June 1992 I got my first professional job at Buffalo General Hospital. Also, around the same time, I met my wife Suzy. She was and always will be one of my biggest supporters.

Things went well those first couple of years at BGH and Suzy and I married in July 1994. Then in late winter of the next year I asked to be taken off the Thioridazine I had been prescribed. I was only taking 10 mg and my psychiatrist acknowledged that it was a "placebo dose". So, I was taken off and within a matter of three weeks was in the middle of another full-blown manic episode. This experience was very traumatic for me and especially Suzy. She was pregnant with our first daughter and now my future appeared to be quite uncertain. I spent a night in Bry Lin Hospital, yet another of Buffalo's mental health treatment facilities, but ended up doing much of my recuperating at my parent's home. Fortunately, I was permitted to return to BGH in June. My daughter Sarah was born two months later.

In January of 1996 I decided that I needed to pursue a career outside of addiction counseling. I was accepted to graduate school at Buffalo State in the Student Personnel Administration Program. I completed the program in 1998 and was hired at Buffalo State in July of that year. My second daughter was born three days after I started working there.

In the 15 years since my last manic episode I have experienced tremendous growth however just because my life has stabilized doesn't mean that life has necessarily gotten easier. There have been numerous stressful moments that have truly tested my sanity. One thing I have learned is that within myself there lays an untapped source of potential, which is where the next chapter begins.

Potential

Merriam-Webster's Dictionary defines the word potential as "existing in possibility."

In its broadest context, this can mean many things. However, when it comes to mental health then I would narrow down this definition to mean reducing one's symptoms and living a life that is productive. Everyone has potential. It's just that one person's potential may not be the same as another's. The key here is not to compare. We all have gifts and talents that can be used.

As I stated earlier, every person is different however there are some common denominators that exist. One of these is the need for hope. We all know what hope is but how many of us, in the grip of our illness, have truly felt it. Hope is the feeling that what is wanted can be had. It is the kind of thing that can be the spark that lights the fire of motivation. One thing that is greatly needed in the lives of the mentally ill is hope. Between the stigma that is placed on the disease and the mental and emotional trauma that is experienced, mentally ill individuals face an uphill battle in the quest for stability. Hope can be a key ingredient in helping us achieve our potential.

When I was first diagnosed 28 years ago, I felt as if there was no hope. I was lost, confused, and afraid. I was afraid of the future that lay ahead and in pain from what I did not understand. My family was feeling much the same. My mother was a trained Rehabilitation Counselor however all of that experience went out the window when it came to dealing with me. I know that she struggled with my illness. She had such high expectations for me and all her hopes for me had been dashed against the rocks.

There were times, in those early days, which I would engage in fantasy about the life I would have one day. I dreamt that I'd have a family, a career, and a home to call my own. You know, the "American Dream". But after a while I began to use these fantasies as a type of visualization exercise. I have read that by visualizing your life as you wanted it to be you could make it a reality. This concept ties into that of potential. By combining the optimism of hope with the possibility of what we can become we are capable of achieving our dreams.

How many of us truly live up to our potential? I mean really. Look at Barack Obama. Now, this is an example of someone who has met his potential. But as I said earlier, we shouldn't compare our own potential with that of others. In my 22 years in a 12-Step program I have seen many individuals who have been able to tap into the potential that lies with them. One of these persons is my friend Chris. Chris was a high school dropout who had a criminal record by the time he was 18. Many called him a hopeless case. He was introduced to a 12-Step program and a miraculous transformation began. Chris restored his relationship with his family; he earned his GED and enrolled in college. He earned his Master's degree and is currently working towards his Ph.D. He is married and has two beautiful children. Chris has learned how to realize the potential that he always had. He embodies the 12-Step message of hope. Self-knowledge supports potential.

When I think of my journey with mental illness, I too see how my potential began to unfold. One key ingredient was ambition. My mother was a big part of this. She never allowed me to settle for second best. She knew when to push hard and when to let up. And along with that I have always had a competitive side. I've always strived to be the best I can be at whatever I'm doing.

One example was in school. During my undergraduate years I struggled academically as well as mentally. One particular semester I earned one B and three Ds. Somehow I managed to earn my Bachelor's degree. Once I got clean I eventually returned to school in an Alcoholism Counselor program. I vividly recall my first exam for a class had in Abnormal Psychology. I earned a grade of 97.5%. I was astonished. This was tangible proof that I had academic potential. I used this experience to motivate myself as I tackled one exam and project after another.

Sometimes, when it comes to mental health, potential simply means staying emotionally stable. Not everyone person who is mentally ill will attend college, or even be able to work for that matter. But wellness is a concept that most can embrace. There is a man named Paul who attends my church. Paul has a diagnosis of schizophrenia. He is in his early 50's. Paul is in attendance every Sunday and it's always a pleasure to see him. As long as I see him in church then I know that things must be okay for him. Paul doesn't work however he has developed a daily routine that works for him. He enjoys music and this is one of the things that help him maintain his equilibrium.

Along with hope, another ingredient in the equation of potential is faith. Faith in a Higher Power supports potential. I believe that faith can help us realize the potential that lies within. Faith is the evidence of things not seen (Hebrews 11:1). We may not have tangible evidence of where our potential lies but with faith we can make it a reality. In a larger sense, the 12-Step framework encourages individuals to believe in a power greater than them. For many, this may be in God, Allah, Buddha, or some other deity. For me, I just choose to call my Higher Power *God*. It is through my faith in God that I can work towards my potential.

I was raised in the church so the concept of God was not hard to grasp. However, when I experienced my first psychotic episode, I began to have difficulty separating belief from delusion. I wasn't able to separate my belief in God from the misperception that my diseased mind created. But this never stopped me from trying to find the truth. During those early years I tried to grasp onto anything that helped me to believe that I could overcome my illness. I would watch everything on TV from Jim and Tammy Faye Bakker to *The 700 Club*. I would try anything to help me believe.

Even when I was institutionalized I would pray. In one instance when I was a patient at the Buffalo Psychiatric Center, I had taken my Bible with me. One evening, I couldn't find it, and after searching, I discovered it in the shower. It had been ruined. I was crushed. I was convinced that the Psych Center was an evil place. In a strange way, this served to reinforce my faith. In my deluded state of mind I was still able to make a connection with God. I knew that God was present in that situation.

We all need something to believe in if we cannot grasp the concept of a Higher Power then we may simply believe in a group. There are support groups in communities nationwide to assist the mentally ill. Later in the book I will elaborate on the concept of support groups. In terms of faith, when things get rough it always helps to have something to believe in.

There are also times when we cannot see the potential that lies within us however there may be someone who can see it for us. Friends, family, clergy, and counselors support potential. I've had help from all of the above.

Like I mentioned earlier, my mother was a tremendous source of encouragement. My father was likewise. Whenever I was hospitalized he would visit me daily. He didn't push like my mother did and his gentle manner of support did wonders. When he entered the doors of the ward he always had a smile on his face and a loving word. He saw my potential.

Then there was Dr. Carrie Johnson. She was a family friend who worked at Buffalo State College as Director of Counseling in the SEEK-EOP program that was designed to assist underrepresented students. Dr. Johnson was from the South - old school. She used to have me over to her house when I was recuperating, to do some basic chores like painting and other projects. She was also instrumental in helping me return to school.

In the fall of 1983 I had just been released from the Psychiatric Center. Dr. Johnson attempted to get me to register for classes at Buffalo State. She literally took me by the hand to the registration hall, but I was unable to commit at the time. The following semester I did register. I firmly believe that if it hadn't been for her assistance I would never have made it. I owe her a debt of gratitude. She saw the potential I had within me.

Reverend Phil Smith was my minister when I was a teen at New Covenant United Church of Christ where I was raised in the Protestant faith. Reverend Smith is a passionate pastor with an incredible knowledge of Christian theology. When I went away to college I left the church physically, but I still had some sense of faith. There were a few occasions when I struggled mentally and in the midst of my confusion would call Reverend Smith in the middle of the night. He would patiently speak to me and provide a prayer. My relationship with him was a crucial part of my recovery. He too saw the potential I had.

Most of my years in early recovery were spent at Horizon Health Services. In the course of 13 years as a client I was counseled by a variety of therapists. Each one of them served as sounding board for whatever issues I happened to be facing at the time. Each one of them saw my potential. As counselors, one part of their job was to help me identify and tap into the potential that lay within me.

In the last 16 years my wife Suzy has helped me realize my potential as much, if not more, than anyone else. Suzy is a very logical person, unlike me.

Whenever I have an idea of a new project she has a very good sense of whether or not it is worth pursuing. If it's something that's completely off the wall she will tell me, or if it is doable then she will agree. I can be somewhat impulsive whereas she is more methodical in her thinking. For instance, in 1998 I took up running as a weight loss exercise. Eight months later when I told her that I wanted to run the Marine Corps Marathon she didn't laugh at me, she gave me her full support. With her help I was able to successfully complete the race. Once again, my potential had been reached.

I feel fortunate to have had the support I have had over the years. I understand that not everyone has that. But that's why it's so important that we learn to recognize our own potential. When we look at our potential we must also recognize our limitations as well.

When I graduated from Buffalo State in 1987 I went to work at a local Buffalo recording studio. My job title was technician. My responsibilities included preparing the studios for recording sessions, assisting sessions, cleaning and running errands. The idea was to have me apprentice so I could eventually record sessions of my own.

Unfortunately, I lacked the technical background that it takes to perform the duties of a recording engineer. So, in a moment of insight I decided to quit the job. I just knew that I didn't have the potential to be an engineer. I realized my limitation in this particular area of my life. At the time it was a bitter pill to swallow but I knew that it would be best if I followed a different career path.

Contrary to the past, I had an experience at Buffalo State College that would affirm the direction I was taking. I was enrolled in my first class in the Student Personnel Administration Program (SPA) at Buffalo State. My professor, Dr. Gallineau, returned the first assigned paper to me with a grade of "A" and a comment that stated, "You have a tremendous potential in the SPA field."

Seeing this comment made me ecstatic. It was like I had discovered gold. When someone validates our healthy choices we feel a sense of hope that can be the spark that ignites a fire within us.

People like Barack Obama are one in a million. But then again, potential can manifest itself in many ways. Potential can simply be a person making it to his counseling appointments consistently or taking on a part-time job successfully. The key thing to remember is that most of us are capable of performing at a higher level than what we think we can. It is possible to move beyond our self-perceived limitations.

WOW Exercise

1) Where would you say your talents lie? What are you good at?

2) Identify at least one person who is able to recognize your talents. Ask him/her to discuss this with you.

3) List the times in your life when you've been emotionally stable. What were the key elements that made this possible?

4) What are your vocational/educational aspirations? How can you achieve them?

The Plan

Every major project needs some kind of a plan or strategy. As I look around my living room I see many examples of planning. From the windows to the entryway, the entire room was initially designed using a blueprint. It is vital to have a plan (or blueprint) for the room/house to be structurally sound. Without it, the house will eventually crumble and fall apart.

The same holds true for those living with mental illness. If we do not have some kind of plan in place then we too will have problems dealing with life. There have been countless self-help books and videos on how to manage mental illness. One of the most recent is the *Wellness Recovery Action Plan* by Mary Ellen Copeland. In her video, Mary Ellen walks the viewer through a simple five-step instructional exercise on how to manage one's mental illness. The video describes the process of Daily Maintenance, Triggers, Early Warning Signs, When Things Break Down and Crisis Plan. The great thing about Dr. Copeland's approach is that it is from someone who has "been there". Her program is easy to follow and is designed to meet the needs of individuals living with mental illness.

For every plan there must be a goal. For the mentally ill it may just be something as simple as remaining out of the hospital. Or it may be returning to work. Whatever the goal, there needs to be some kind of strategy to achieve the desired result. In my career as a counselor I have been accustomed to creating treatment plans for the clients with whom I work. One of the most valuable lessons I have learned was that clients benefit most when they participate in the treatment planning process. Instead of creating arbitrary objectives, I draw my clients into the process thereby empowering them. This allowed my clients to be a part of their own plan to achieve a sense of stability in their lives. When we, as consumers, are involved in treatment planning, we become actively engaged, and thereby improve our chances of succeeding.

The same thing happened for me when my counselor Dick gave me those three options back in 1988 when I decided to attend the 12-Step meeting. I had to make the decision, on my own, which way I wanted to go. Thank goodness I chose the path of recovery. Through this decision I was also held accountable for my actions. Accountability is crucial when creating a plan. In the end, we must live up to our own expectations for ourselves.

Another valuable tool that goes hand-in-hand with the planning process is self-assessment. How else will we know what we are capable of unless we take an honest look at ourselves? We can do this with the help of others. Family, friends or our mental health professionals can help us to take such an inventory. One of the first things we need to ask ourselves is, "How did I get to where I'm at today?"

To get to where we are going we need to know where we've been. It is important at this time to examine oneself and look for any patterns in our lives that may emerge. It would be helpful to write this information down. Many people, including myself, have used journals to chronicle events in their lives. Journals can clearly identify the times in our lives when we have encountered trouble as well as been successful at dealing with stressors. Once we have some kind of reference to our past we can more objectively determine our own potential as well as limitations.

Having a written plan can make a huge difference in guiding our actions. For one, when we have a written plan, we have something to help us along the way. In the same respect, chronicling the experience through journaling is a way of helping us to be accountable for our actions. This is your plan and no one else's. At the end of the day when we jot down the events of our day we are able to see how well we have done in terms of reaching our goal.

Remember the last chapter? The concept of potential is tied directly to that of self-assessment. We would never want to create a goal for ourselves that is unrealistic. This is simply a recipe for failure. Goals should be "doable" without being unrealistic. For instance, when I started running twelve years ago, my goal was simply to run 20 minutes without any significant pain. Once I accomplished this I began to push my limits in terms of the distance I could run and the time that it took. It is important to go beyond our comfort zone once we have achieved our initial goal.

So, the first thing you need to do is to determine goals for the different areas of your life. Let's say you're a smoker and your goal is to quit. You may want to explore the different kind of smoking cessation programs that are available. Once you find one then you can set a daily goal of minimizing your cigarette use. Remember, when setting goals our plan should be broken down to a one day at a time type of method. It is often easier to manage something for one day than it is to expect to do so for a longer period of time or forever, for instance.

The one general goal we may have is to remain out of the hospital therefore we may need to employ a variety of strategies in our plan. One crucial issue is medication management. A related strategy may be dealing with side effects. Unfortunately many psychotropic medications do have adverse side effects. Lethargy and weight gain are often considered to be problematic for those taking these kinds of drugs. One way to counter these effects is to stay active. Even a brisk walk can do wonders when we are feeling sluggish. I'll be addressing exercise in a later chapter.

Another tool we can employ when implementing our plan is communication. It is vitally important that we keep the lines of communication open with our supporters. These supporters can be family, friends, or mental health professionals. When these lines of communication break down, we are more vulnerable, thereby making us more susceptible to an episode - whether it is manic, depressive, psychotic, or otherwise.

One valuable method that Mary Ellen Copeland outlines in the *Wellness Recovery Action Plan is* the Crisis Plan. In the Crisis Plan, Copeland instructs us to write out a plan that can be given to five of our supporters that outlines what steps should be taken in the case of a psychiatric episode. Through the use of a crisis plan we are able to let our supporters know how we should be handled when we may not be capable of communicating effectively for ourselves.

It is also important to find someone we can trust. This is vital. When I was struggling mentally, I often felt that I had no one I could talk to or understood what I was going through. I felt like I was alone. In retrospect, there were people in my life I could talk to however I did not trust them with my thoughts and feelings. I had many people trying to help me: parents, friends, and counselors. Unfortunately, I was incapable of understanding that their actions were simply meant to reach me in my diminished state.

Peer-based support groups such as "Double Trouble" have gained considerable acceptance and popularity. One of the key ingredients that contribute to the success of peer support groups is that of empathy. Empathy is defined as, "understanding and entering into another's feelings," or "putting oneself into another's shoes."

The Depression Bipolar Support Alliance (DBSA) is a nationwide organization that has branched out to the internet to bring mentally ill persons closer together. There are hundreds, if not thousands of mental health-related resources online. The main caution I would offer is that you practice caution when reviewing mental health information on the internet. It would be wise to go over any treatments you may find with your counselor to ensure that they are in your best interest. Besides the DBSA, I would also recommend Mental Health America (MHA), NAMI (National Alliance on Mental

Illness) or SAMHSA (Substance Abuse & Mental Health Services Administration).

When I joined a 12-Step program in 1988 I finally felt like I was with people who knew what I was dealing with. Not only did they have substance abuse problems but also there were those challenged by mental health disorders. When I heard others openly sharing their feelings about their illness I became comfortable with doing the same.

There is an age-old saying that says, "Know thy self." That's a big part of what *Working on Wellness* is all about. We are all individuals with different needs and what might work for one may not work for another. What is important to understand is that the fundamental concepts of wellness apply to everyone no matter what the situation. For example, I was finally diagnosed with bipolar disorder in 1983. My life back then was filled with alcohol and illicit drug use, as well as medication mismanagement. It was no wonder I could not stay out of the hospital for long. It was not until I had a plan in place to address the drugs and properly take my meds that my situation began to improve. The key to my success was that I made the decision to surrender and try things a different way. I had no clue what wellness was but I was beginning to practice some of the principles found with this new way of life. Eventually, things began to get better. My symptoms slowly began to disappear, my physical health improved, and my spiritual life blossomed. I began to experience a life that I never knew existed.

Another maxim is "If you fail to plan, you plan to fail." This concept is especially true when it comes to mental wellness. Due to the nature of our disease we need to have a routine to follow to enhance our chance of remaining symptom free. This is where Copeland's WRAP principle of Daily Maintenance comes into play. She recommends that we write down the day-to-day tasks we do when we are doing well. Things such as taking our meds, bathing and hygiene, and eating three meals a day are all important in developing a healthy routine.

There are times when the idea of creating a plan may be overwhelming. "Where do I begin? Where do I start?" The answer is relatively simple. Just think about what you can do today to lead a healthy life. Chances are you probably know what some of these things are. As I stated previously, it is important to be realistic when creating your plan. And don't forget...this is your plan and no one else's.

WOW Exercise

1)   Think of a goal you would like to accomplish. Is it realistic? Write it down.

2)   What are some of the tools you have in place to accomplish it?

3)   Who are some of the people that can help you reach your goal?

4)   What is a realistic timeframe in which you can accomplish your goal?

Wellness Recovery Action Plan (WRAP) – www.mentalhealthrecovery.com
Depression Bipolar Support Alliance (DBSA) - www.dbsalliance.org
Mental Health America (MHA) – www.nmha.org
Substance Abuse & Mental Health Services Administration (SAMHSA) - www.samhsa.gov
Wellness Recovery Action Plan - www.mentalhealthrecovery.com

The Spirit Within

Spirituality is one of the cornerstone elements of wellness. This is the part of the recovery equation that is crucial. Why? Because without some kind of spiritual element present it can be very difficult to cope with life's many problems, not to mention having a mental illness.

When I first became ill in 1981, along with receiving psychiatric care, I also received spiritual therapy. Having been raised in the church, my family utilized almost every kind of religious method possible to bring me out of my struggle. I remember entering my mother's bedroom and seeing her watching *The 700 Club*. She also referred me to a family friend who acted as a spiritual mentor during this period. Faith and prayer were a constant in my life however in the beginning I struggled to find something to believe in.

I know, without any hesitation, that my spiritual practices have greatly helped me to manage my bipolar disorder. Even during the times when my illness produced delusional behavior I still prayed, believing that a power greater than myself could restore me to sanity. All of us have this unlimited resource at our disposal.

If hope is the spark, then faith is the fire. Faith is so important for those struggling with mental illness. We are people who so often have so much of life stacked against us. Whether it is hospitalization, anxiety, or depression, faith is required just to get us through the day. There are so many ways in which we can practice our spirituality. In fact, that is the beautiful thing, there's something for everyone. Another consideration is that being spiritual does not necessarily equate to being religious. Some people may have never stepped into a church or any other religious structure but they are still capable of living a spiritual life.

So, once again, why is spirituality so important to those living with mental illness? Well, if we are able to find something loving and caring and greater than us, then we can become capable of learning to love ourselves. If I can say that God loves me then I can find a sense of belonging that says that life can become more bearable. Belief in a higher power can help us to face any challenge that comes our way.

The parable of the mustard seed has been evident in my life in so many ways. This parable is told by Jesus in Matthew 17-20: "Because of your lack of faith, I tell you with certainty, if you have faith like a grain of mustard seed, you can say to this mountain, 'Move from here to there,' and it will move, and nothing will be impossible for you."

Where do we begin with finding our spiritual compass? Believe it or not it isn't as difficult as you may think. One way is to say a prayer. It can be as simple as saying, "God help me," but done on a deep feeling level. It is important to remember that you cannot intellectualize spirituality. It has to come from the heart.

One prayer that is commonly used in 12-Step programs is the Serenity Prayer:

"God grant me the serenity to accept the things I cannot change; courage to change the things I can; and wisdom to know the difference."

This simple devotion has worked in thousands, if not millions, of people's lives. It too can work for those living with mental disorders. Serenity is something that we all can use. When it comes to accepting that we have a mental illness, it can be difficult to face this unfortunate reality. By tapping into the power greater than ourselves we are able to get through anything.

In 1994 I had to have surgery to remove all of my wisdom teeth. I was very nervous and apprehensive about this procedure. Much of my concern was due to the general anesthesia that I would have to be under to have the extractions done. I was trapped in the memory of receiving anesthesia for ECT (shock therapy) twelve years earlier. In order to get through this experience I had to employ the Serenity Prayer. I knew that I couldn't change the fact that I had to have the teeth taken out so I had to accept it. In the end I came through with flying colors. I used this experience at other times to remind me that God was with me.

Acceptance also means that we do not have to settle for a life that is disconnected from the world around us. By accepting our illness we can then be able to look at ourselves and honestly see who we are. Remember the concept of potential. If we accept ourselves, then we see not only our limitations, but also begin to get a glimpse of our potential.

Courage is a vital element. Remember the Cowardly Lion in *The Wizard of Oz*? All he needed to do was realize that he already had courage. We too have demonstrated courage just by virtue of living with mental illness. Just being able to wake up and face every day is a brave act. By incorporating a life of faith and prayer we develop courage that is not our own.

Wisdom many times comes from the ability to discern God's will for us. Many times wisdom comes when I am faced with a difficult decision or challenge, I simply pray, "Your will be done, not mine." In the end, as my sponsor Dave says, "God's will for us is in hindsight." That's where past experience comes into play If we are leading a spiritual life, we can look back and see how things have worked out and determine if the way we acted was in accordance with God's will. I believe that we may have some kind of inkling as to what God's will is for us; it is just up to us to act on that intuitive decision.

There may be times with some psychiatric disorders that individuals may have a skewed sense of religion or spirituality. This is where help may be needed. When I was in the throes of my manic episodes I would often experience delusions and religious preoccupation. Many times I thought I was Jesus and that I had mystical powers. I would engage in ritualistic behaviors, bizarre writing, and drawing. When this happened my family and friends intervened to get me the help I needed. This is why it is vital that when exploring a spiritual path, those with mental illness "keep their feet on the ground." How, you may ask? By remaining connected with our social supports. Counselors, family, and friends can all assist us when we are trying to find our way. If we begin to go in the wrong direction, our supporters can be there to help keep our thinking back on track. Also, it is vital that we stay on our medication regimen. This is where many individuals have difficulty. When we are feeling good it is easy to think that we don't need to take medication.

In 1995, when I had my most recent manic episode, I had gotten heavily involved with a mystical fraternal organization. This particular group was into exploring metaphysical concepts as well as other spiritual practices. What I failed to realize was that this kind of activity was not in my best interest. It simply took me out too far. When this happened though, I was fortunate to have a family that rallied around me. My wife was five months pregnant so I had a lot on the line. I was also working as addictions counselor at a local healthcare facility. Somehow, by the grace of God, I managed to get through this traumatic experience. I was out of work for three months and during this time I leaned heavily on those around me.

What do we do if we don't have a viable family support system? Then it's time to seek out help from external sources. As I previously mentioned, support groups can be a tremendously valuable venue for getting help. When we can enter a room of people with whom we have something in common then we can feel that we are accepted and that we belong. Remember the saying, "It takes one to know one." It is especially true with mental illness. When you have experienced the pain and trauma associated with mental disorders, it is important to know that you could talk to someone who has been there. Through this experience we experience the intrinsic spiritual element of empathy –understanding and entering into another's feelings. Family is not just constructed from our blood relatives. As an only child I grew up without experiencing what it means to have siblings but in my life today I have friends that I can call brothers and sisters. By having true friends we can develop a true sense of spirituality.

There may also be times when we are alone and have to tap into the spirit within. I have another more recent example of when this was the case in my life. In 2007, I went to China on a business trip. This was my second experience going to the Far East and things had gone well; at least until the flight back. I left Nanjing after having gotten up at 5 a.m. and flew to Hong Kong. The flight from Hong Kong was 14 hours long. I arrived safely in Chicago and was prepared for the final leg back to Buffalo. As it turned out, there were a number of tornado watches in the Northern Midwest and Northeast. My flight ended up being cancelled and with the luck of having met up with a couple of fellow Buffalonians, I was able to secure a hotel room. Unfortunately, I had left all my medication in my luggage that was back at the airport. By this time I had been up for about 27 hours with no sleep. I tried to relax but I was unable to sleep. I began to worry. In the past, lack of sleep had been a major trigger for my manic episodes.

Finally, I decided to reach into the bedside table and pull out the Gideon Bible. Without any specific thought I opened it up and I looked down. It was in the Book of Matthew 11:28, "Come to me all who are weary and laden and I will give you rest." When I read this I knew that everything would be okay. I knew it in my heart. From there I was able to relax, and although I didn't sleep, I made it through the night and then onto the flight home. This experience reinforces for me the power of faith in coping with mental illness.

Another means in which some people explore spirituality is through meditation. When many people think of meditation they visualize someone sitting in the lotus position chanting "Om." In reality, meditation is a way in which those with mental illness can take a few moments to wind down and find a little peace within them. Meditation does not necessarily have to be for a long period of time. Even five minutes can be enough to tap into that inner reserve.

To start, simply find a quiet place. Some people use soothing music. Sit with your back straight and both feet on the floor. Slowly inhale and exhale for about a minute. Then, slowly, tense and relax your muscles starting at your feet and then work your way up the body. As you tense each section inhale as you tense each muscle group and then exhale as you release. If you are not comfortable doing this with your eyes closed then alternate for a minute or so with them open.

In some meditative practices, the use of a mantra is employed. A mantra is a word or phrase, that when used, has the ability to center oneself and deepen your connection with your higher power. One example is "Lord Jesus have mercy on me" or "Om Mani Padme Hum"(jewel in the lotus of the heart).

Through the use of meditation we can realize physical benefits as well. Meditation has been proven to lower blood pressure. If you develop this practice you will quickly realize positive results. You may have difficulty at first, but with persistence, you will be able to find what method works for you.

So, as you can see, there are many ways in which we can nurture our spirituality. Please bear in mind the importance of having a spiritual partner; someone with whom we can "check in" about our spiritual practice. The key is that it is important to be patient. Even the greatest spiritual beings spent a life time refining their practice. On the other hand, even saying something as simple as the Serenity Prayer can do wonders for helping you connect with your higher power.

WOW Exercise

1) Have you practiced any religious or spiritual path? If so, briefly describe it.

2) Identify one person who can be your spiritual partner. Connect with him/her and share your spiritual journey.

3) Select a prayer, no matter what the religious tradition, and use it to connect with your higher power.

4) Recall a time when you relied on your spiritual connection to help you through a difficult situation.

5) Regularly take time to meditate in the method you feel comfortable. Be sure not to go longer than 15 minutes when you start. If you find yourself falling asleep, that's okay.

The Mind-Body Connection

Wellness is comprised of the mental, physical, and spiritual. Each of these components is closely intertwined. When those who are living with mental illness are faced with challenges such as stabilizing on medication, or maintaining an emotional equilibrium, one area that is often overlooked is their physical condition. What I'll be looking at in this chapter is how the body can affect the mind and vice-versa.

Our society is a study in contradiction. On the one hand, the media tells us that we need to lose weight through any number of means while on the other hand we have to put up with a constant barrage of food commercials. The result is a mixed message that ends up leaving us confused and many times frustrated. For individuals living with mental health disorders these messages can be equally, if not more confusing. What is important for us to know is how vital taking care of our bodies is when it comes to our mental health. Studies have shown a direct correlation between chronic mental illness and diminished life expectancy. (Mentally ill die 25 years earlier on average, Elias, May 3, 2007).

There has been scientific research that supports the argument that exercise can improve one's mental health. These findings validate what I have experienced first-hand. In 1998, I was starting a new job and my physical health was probably the worst it had ever been. I weighed nearly 220 pounds and I began to get worried. I had watched my mother's health suffer as a result of poor diet and no exercise. She died much too soon at the age of 66.

So, I made the decision to try getting into shape. My job as a college recruiter took me on the road so I figured this was a perfect opportunity to take advantage of hotel fitness rooms. On October 23, I tied up my running shoes and hit the treadmill. I took it slow but I was able to run 20 minutes without any significant aches or pains. This was all I needed to get me going. I was able to run 3-4 times per week for about a half-hour or so. Within a short period of time I began to see the pounds disappear. But just as importantly, I noticed my general mood improve as well. Scientific research supports this evidence as well:"Exercise may be a positive adjunct for the treatment of depression since exercise provides additional health benefits (e.g., increase in muscle tone and decreased incidence of heart disease and obesity) that behavioral interventions do not." (The influence of Exercise on Mental Health, Landers, December 1997).

One example in my life was when I decided to take up running at the age of 36. I was in dire need of a fitness program. I had the experience of running when I was a senior in high school and even earned a varsity letter in cross-country and track. So looking back on my past performance I knew that I had some ability to run. I undertook my new running program and before I knew it I was hooked. I lost nearly 50 pounds and was running 4-5 times per week. The following year I ran the Marine Corps Marathon with the Team in Training (TNT) Program of the Leukemia and Lymphoma Society. As part of TNT I took part in an 18-week running program. The program consisted of running various distances 5 times per week concluding with a long run on Saturday mornings. This plan was instrumental in assisting my fellow TNT runners and me. Without this plan I probably never could have completed the 26.2 mile race.

There are many forms of physical exercise that can be beneficial. The key is to find one that can be performed regularly and that suits your lifestyle.

Now, before I go any further, I should stress the point that if you are considering taking on an exercise routine that you get checked out by your physician first. Once you get the okay to begin, then you will know that type of work out is best for you.

Another thing that bears mentioning is that there are many ways to exercise. Running obviously is not the only way to get in shape. Everything from walking to cycling to swimming can be a benefit to one's health. One benefit of walking is that it is an easy form of exercise to access (you can do it virtually anywhere) and there is virtually no cost involved.

Another thing that helps is to get a workout partner. By having someone to exercise with we are more likely to follow through with our plans. An additional benefit to this method is that we are less likely to isolate. Some of my best workouts were completed in the company of friends. All it takes is 3-4 times per week for one-half hour.

Since I started my exercise program in 1998 I haven't had any significant periods of depression.

Exercise has proven to be the perfect complement to my prescribed medications in keeping me emotionally stable. I have had the experience on numerous occasions of finishing a workout and feeling the immediate gratification of endorphins firing off in my brain. Really, I'm serious. Exercise has been linked to an increase in endorphins which are a naturally occuring chemical in the brain. They're kind of like a natural mood lifter. This beats the heck out of the illicit drugs I used to use for the same effect.

One final positive aspect of exercise is how it relates to goal setting. There is a tremendous amount of satisfaction and confidence that goes along with setting a goal and achieving it. It does wonders for one's self esteem.

Smoking is a negative habit that greatly impacts many who live with mental illness. It is the cause of heart disease, cancer, and emphysema, to name but a few health conditions. Harvard researchers found that "41 percent of people with mental illness are smokers compared to 22.5 percent of people who have never been mentally ill. (Smoking and Mental Illness – A Prevalence Based Study, Lasser, MD et al, November 2000). These days it is impossible to get away from all the anti-smoking literature and advertisements that warn of the dangers of smoking. Unfortunately, these messages are still not enough to convince some people to quit. Smoking is an addiction and should be treated as such. There are many types of smoking cessation programs available to those who want to quit. Whether it is nicotine patches, gum, or alternative methods such as acupuncture, quitting is more of a possibility than it has ever been before.

I would also strongly recommend having an annual physical and seeking your doctor's recommendations on how to improve your physical health. Nutrition is another crucial element of the wellness equation. It is far too easy to give in to the temptations of our fast food culture. The key is moderation. There are plenty of healthy alternatives which will help you to feel better and live longer.

Finally, you should keep an open dialogue with your psychiatrist about the medication(s) you are taking. Many psych meds have side effects. It may take a little while to find the right one(s) for you as well as the proper dosage. The best way to find out is to tell your psychiatrist what side effects you may be experiencing.

In the early days of my illness I was prescribed everything from Thorazine to Haldol, Stelazine, Navane, Artane, and the list goes on. It took about two years before it was determined that I had bipolar disorder and Lithium was prescribed.

When it comes to wellness, the physical component is as equally important as the emotional and spiritual. The way we feel physically directly affects these other areas. For instance, if we have diabetes, we can be affected emotionally, perhaps by becoming depressed over our condition. The thing to remember is that by taking care of our physical health, our overall emotional state will be more inclined to improve.

As I stated, our physical and emotional health are intrinsically linked. If you've ever been depressed, then you know what I mean. In the summer of 1983 I was clinically depressed. I was so out of it that I was incapable of even getting out of bed or taking a shower. I even found no pleasure in listening to music, which was highly unusual. As a result of this episode I ended up spending about a month in the Buffalo Psychiatric Center. I did recover, albeit briefly. Looking back on this experience, I am still amazed at how little physical energy I had. Fortunately, I have been able to identify the times when I am sliding down emotionally and take the appropriate steps to get better.

There are medications available that can help with symptoms of depression. Three important reminders are to take them as prescribed, report any negative side effects to your physician, and absolutely do not mix them with alcohol or any illicit drugs. Anti-depressants can help however they need to be closely monitored.

Finally, I've learned an awful lot over the years about what works well for me in terms of how my mind and body work together. One of the most important things I've learned is that there are some things that work for everyone (exercise of some kind) while there are other things that are specific to the individual (types of medications). The point is that you need to find what works for you. And as the old saying goes, "If it ain't broke don't fix it." If you see that something is working right, by all means keep it up. On the other hand, if it isn't, then maybe there needs to be an adjustment. In the end, with patience and persistence, you will find your way.

WOW Exercise

1) Get a physical to ensure that you are capable of exercising at a level suited for your ability.

2) Identify one form of exercise to practice for 3-4 times per week for a half hour

3) Do you smoke? If so, talk to your physician about getting a nicotine replacement treatment.

Broussard-Wilson, Samantha, Yale Daily News, Study finds link between exercise, mental health October 2007.

Elias, Marilyn, USA Today, Mentally ill die 25 years earlier on average, May 3,2007.

Landers, Daniel M., The Influence of Exercise on Mental Health, Series 2, Number 12 PCPFS Research Digest December 1997.

Lasser, Karen MD; Boyd, J. Wesley MD, PhD; Woolhandler, Steffie MD, MPH; Himmelstein, David U. MD; McCormick, Danny MD, MPH; Bor, David H. MD, Smoking and Mental Illness A Population-Based Prevalence Study *JAMA.* 2000;284:2606-2610.

A Shoulder to Lean On

Another component of the wellness equation is support. Support can come in the form of family or friends. We need people in our lives for a variety of reasons. One such place where we can seek out help is support groups. When it comes to those who are living with mental illness and addiction, support groups can often fill the gap left open by family or friends that may not be able to provide the time needed to help us.

There are many reasons why support groups are so valuable. The first is that they can provide a caring atmosphere of empathy. It is through empathy that we are able to get in tune with each other's true feelings. It can make all the difference in feeling a part of the group.

A key turning point in my life was when I went to my first 12-Step meeting. I was nervous and afraid of what to expect. When I walked through the door and was given a welcoming hug by the greeter, I immediately felt better. Then, once I began to hear the open and honest sharing of some of the group members, I was able to relate and realized I was in the right place. It was through the atmosphere of empathy that I found in the rooms of recovery that I was able to develop a trusting relationship with my fellow recovering addicts.

Learning to trust is an important part of finding a support group. It is vital that we feel safe and comfortable with those around us. This is difficult for some. One way to deal with this sense of discomfort is to take slow steps in becoming a part of the group. The first thing to try is simply listening. By listening to others share it is possible to gauge how trustworthy the group is as a whole. Also, it's not like you need to share your deepest darkest secret. It can be something as simple as how your day is going or even providing feedback on what other group members may share. Active listening allows us to not only hear what someone else is saying but it also helps us to empathize.

Once again, for me, my experience at that first twelve-step meeting is an example of how listening to others share allowed me to trust the group process. That evening a young woman was celebrating 30 days clean. She expressed her frustration and anger at how her life had become. I was amazed that someone who was capable of abstaining from drugs and alcohol for 30 days could be so angry. What I was able to get from her open honesty was the sense that I could feel safe expressing how I really felt. It was so often in the past that I found it necessary to stuff my feelings. The atmosphere of recovery that I experienced was something new for me.

Another aspect of support groups I need to talk about is how we relate to each other. More specifically, I am referring to the idea that when people are among others like themselves, they will use terminology that is best understood by others like themselves. "It takes one to know one" is an example of what I mean. This is the primary reason why the peer movement has seen such phenomenal growth. This may happen in group therapy with the help of a counselor, however in a peer-based setting the sense that we are all battling the same common illness can be a tremendous tool. It is through one person relating to another that we find a true sense of empathy. There is an expression that states, "Pain shared is pain eased." This couldn't be more true. When we find a place where we can openly share our struggles, we can learn from others who have experienced the same hurts.

Friendship is yet another byproduct of joining a support group. Many of us who enter treatment have not experienced true friendship. What I mean by this is that often times our lives have been characterized by false friendships; ones that are not open and honest.

When I was actively using drugs and alcohol many, if not most, of my friendships were based on what the other person could do for me, and vice-versa. Unfortunately, the haze of addiction and delusion I experienced kept me from seeing how flawed these so-called friendships were. Over time, I have learned who my true friends are.

When I got involved in 12-Step recovery, I learned the value of what true friendship was all about. In March 1995 my life was spiraling out of control. One evening I found myself distraught, crying, and frightened. I was in the midst of another manic episode. My wife asked me what I wanted her to do. "Call Mark," I replied. He was one of my friends who I met in the rooms of recovery. She called Mark, who lived a half-hour away. Without any hesitation, he drove to my North Buffalo home and took me to a twelve-step meeting. Mark, and many of my other twelve-step friends, helped me through that difficult time. Without them, I don't think that my recovery would have progressed so quickly. This was the last manic episode I ever experienced.

Another offshoot of support groups is the ability to find activities that you may have in common with others. This is one of the great things about support groups. We can find many interests that we share with others. You might just find someone who shares a similar affectation for music or sports or books, for instance. You never know. When I met my sponsor Dave, I quickly learned that he enjoyed shooting pool. It just so happened that I had a pool table. We spent many hours in the early days playing together. In fact, we even played snooker during one of our trips to Toronto! It was during these times that our relationship grew. The shared activity served as a vehicle for us to become closer.

Support groups are also a means in which we can realize that we are not unique. I cannot tell you the number of times over the years that I've heard someone shares an aspect of his or her life that I have experienced. By eliminating our uniqueness, we can no longer use the lame excuse of saying, "But you don't understand me!"

It's hard to hide behind our uniqueness when there's someone else sharing an experience or feeling that we too have had. I vividly recall hearing other addicts in the rooms of recovery who also struggled with mental illness. Their sharing of how they had difficulty remaining balanced was something I could relate to. I had for so long thought that I was the only one who dealt with such erratic instability. When others shared their experience it helped me to learn from them. These were some of the greatest lessons I have ever had.

WOW Exercise

1) Have you ever had experience with a support group? If so, describe it.

2) Have you had the experience of talking with someone who "got you" or understood you? If so, whom and how did you know?

3) Are there any support groups in your area that you would consider attending? If so, which ones?

If you are unsure of support groups in your area consider visiting an online community such as the Depression Bipolar Support Alliance (DBSA - www.dbsalliance.org) to find one in your area.

Working on Work

One of the hallmarks of mental health stability is the ability to hold a job. For many who live with mental illness this is an elusive goal. There are several things that can contribute to a meaningful transition to the world of work.

Often times, when we start a new job we have to learn new things. Going to work can mean stepping out of one's comfort zone. While this may appear to be an anxiety-provoking prospect, it doesn't necessarily have to be. By starting off slowly, the process can be more manageable.

If you have had a limited work history or have never worked before, you may want to consider volunteering. Volunteer work is great for those who may want to test the waters. There are many agencies that need volunteers. If you are unsure of where to find one, you can contact the United Way in your area. You can also volunteer in an area that would look good on your resume, or that you enjoy a lot – just identify and approach the non-profit, or more rarely, for-profit business and ask if they use volunteers.

If you happen to currently be in an outpatient treatment program you certainly should take advantage of any vocational rehabilitation services that are available. When I was a client at Horizon Health Services I took part in one of their early Job Club groups. I was also linked with the NY State Office of Vocational Rehabilitation (now called

Vocational Educational Services for Individuals with Disabilities or VESID).

The Job Club helped me with the basics of learning how to write a resume and prepare for an interview among other things. It also taught me how to be responsible and show up consistently which is a trait that I still hold onto today.

The next step in the vocational process may be temporary employment. Temporary employment agencies hire individuals to work for a limited period of time for companies. As opposed to volunteer positions, temp jobs are usually paid experiences.

In my early recovery I had the opportunity to work for a local temporary employment agency. During my time there I was able to work in two law firms, a print shop, and the Buffalo IRS office. Each of the jobs I held was perfect for me at the time. Due to my temporary status, I did not feel overwhelmed by the prospect of losing my job due to my performance. On the other hand, each of these jobs required me to be on time and fulfill the responsibilities that were expected. I had to be accountable. Another positive aspect was that I felt like I was contributing to society. For many years prior to this I relied on Public Assistance and SSI to support myself. There's nothing quite like receiving a paycheck that you have worked for.

Another avenue to employment is school. Education has always been a means to improve one's station in life, and rightly so. It has been proven that the more education you have, the more employable you will be. Also, those with college degrees typically earn more than their high school degree counterparts.

Since the advent of the Americans with Disabilities Act, education for those living with mental illness has become a possibility for millions. Now, more than ever, the dream of an education can be a reality.

There are many venues in which one can pursue an education depending on one's career goal. For some, this may be clear. For others a little help is required. If you are in need of preparation for college you may want to consider attending a pre-collegiate educational program. In Buffalo, where I live, the Educational Opportunity Center is one place where individuals can take classes that will prepare them for the rigors of college-level study. In fact, my mother worked there for several years and I recall her stories of some of the successful students she had the opportunity to help out.

Another educational option is community college. These types of schools offer programs that will allow an individual to enter directly into the workplace as well as those which provide for a seamless transition into a four-year program. Community colleges also offer academic support for those who may be in need of assistance with math, reading, and/or English proficiency.

In 1990 I attended Erie Community College (ECC) to take the courses I needed for my substance abuse credential. This program was every bit as rigorous as any other college course I have taken. I also had the experience of working at Genesee Community College several years ago and I was able to witness, first hand, the value of a community college education. As a rule, community colleges have an open admissions policy, meaning that as long as you have a high school degree, or equivalent, you have to be admitted. Also, tuition at community colleges is typically less expensive than most four-year schools. But do not be fooled. A community college education can lead to great things. As I previously stated, you just have to be willing to step out of your comfort zone.

Somehow I managed to graduate with my Bachelor's degree from Buffalo State. My undergraduate years were a classic combination of delusion and addiction. There were times when my illness caused me to stop in order to be hospitalized only to return to school and have the cycle continue over and over again. My grades were inconsistent. My future was unclear. When I finally got clean and had a period of stability, I made the decision to attend ECC. I was quite concerned about my ability to handle the academic rigor of the classes I was scheduled to take due to my past history. What I quickly found was that I was more focused and driven to succeed. Although I didn't earn straight "A's" I did complete the program which led to me landing a job in my chosen field.

So, what do you do if you want to go to school but don't know what kind of job to pursue? Well, most colleges have career placement offices that can assist you with a variety of career related decisions. These offices are equipped with computer-based software that can help with the career exploration process. They are sometimes called career interest inventories. Basically, what these programs do is to have you reply to a series of questions and match your answers to those of others who are employed in a wide range of jobs. These inventories can be very helpful and they are a valuable tool in the job search process. In addition, the staff is skilled at helping students identify potential career paths. All you have to do is ask for their help, their services are free. You can also find a variety of career inventories online.

Career placement offices can also assist you with things such as resume writing, mock interviews, and job placement. They may also conduct job fairs where companies visit the campus to recruit potential employees. When I was working on my Master's degree at Buffalo State I often visited the Career Development Center to conduct my job search. I found the staff to be knowledgeable and they were able to provide me with the assistance that I needed.

Another important office for those who are living with mental illness is the Disabilities Services Office. Like the career center, disabilities offices are found on all college campuses. These offices assist students that may require accommodations to complete their academic program. One thing that is required is an evaluation by a licensed psychologist. This evaluation needs to show a marked impairment in psychological functioning. By reviewing the proper diagnosis, disabilities office personnel will then determine which special accommodations are appropriate for each student. These can be provisions such as extended test time, separate location, or a reader. Accommodations are a legal right for students with disabilities. If you feel that you may require accommodations then the disabilities office should be one of your first stops on campus. Essentially, they are designed to "level the playing field" for students with disabilities.

One point I should mention is that if you are, or have been, in high school and had an Individualized Education Plan (IEP), the laws in college are different. In high school your parents could advocate for you and you may have received special treatment in your classes. The main thing to remember is that in college you have to be your own advocate. The Family Education Right to Privacy Act (FERPA) is a federal law that prevents parents from viewing or obtaining students' records (without a special waiver). This simply means that you have to be the one to let the school, by way of the disabilities office, know that you are in need of accommodations.

Oddly enough, when I was studying as an undergraduate I never utilized the services of the Disabilities Services Office. In retrospect, I really wish I had. When I think of how I struggled to maintain my classes and just get by, I now know that I could have used the help of the staff there. There's no shame in asking for help. This is another important part of wellness.

At Genesee Community College I supervised the Disabilities Services staff. It never ceased to amaze me how compassionate they were and how much they genuinely cared for the students who came to their office for help. The Disabilities Services Office at GCC, as well as those at other colleges, provides an invaluable service.

With all of my years of college-related experience, both as a student and as an employee, I have realized one thing. Getting a college degree isn't always as much a matter of intelligence as it is a matter of hard work and persistence. The students that succeed in college are those who know how to balance their many responsibilities and DON'T GIVE UP! However, if you find yourself having difficulty keeping it together, by all means, don't just stop going to class. If you do so you run the risk of doing irreparable damage to your academic record. There is a proper way of withdrawing from classes. This is, once again, where the Disabilities Services Office can be of assistance.

So come on, step out of that comfort zone. Remember the chapter on potential? You have abilities you will never know unless you take that healthy risk. All it takes is desire and drive. And another thing – don't ever let anyone tell you that you can't do it. If I had listened to such people along the way I would never be where I am today.

WOW Exercise

1)   Do you have a job or career that you always dreamed of pursuing?   If so, what is it?

2)   Are there any volunteer opportunities that interest you? Make a list of agencies that you can contact to explore your options.

3)   Are you interested in attending college? Make an appointment to meet with an admissions counselor to discuss the application process.

4)   Do you have an interest in going to work? Identify a specific job that you'd like to do and contact a company that employs these kinds of workers.

The Journey Continues

There is an ancient proverb that says, "The journey of a thousand miles begins with the first step." This is where it all begins. Wellness is not as much a destination as it is a journey. The whole idea is to find out what makes us tick. As I stated previously, what works for one person may not work for another. What I have attempted to do is to provide you with practical examples of how to grow as a person and develop the skills to make your life a little bit better. So, as the saying goes, "Take what you need and leave the rest behind."

In my journey of recovery I have met so many people who live with mental illness that have become successful and stable. I'm not saying that it has necessarily been easy for them (or for me for that matter). If anything, the journey to wellness can be a difficult one otherwise how would we be able to fully appreciate what we have earned.

Potential, support, spirituality, physical and emotional health are all parts of the wellness journey. Add to that the aspect of vocational and educational aspiration and you get the possibility of a life you have never known.

When embarking on this journey we have to be prepared to face our fears and work through them. We do this by practicing faith in our higher power. We also have to take those healthy risks in small, manageable doses. Once we are successful at overcoming these initial obstacles we can become more confident in our ability to tackle the larger ones.

Finally, my mother always told me to be the best at whatever I tried to do. And that is the challenge that I give to you. No matter what it is you do, do the best you can. Not the best someone else can, but the best you can. As long as you put forth your best effort you can have the satisfaction that you gave it your all. It's up to you.

CPSIA information can be obtained at www.ICGtesting.com
260289BV00001B/8/P